Watch Out, Freddy, Muffles, and Percy!

by Christel Kleitsch and Joyce Zemke
Illustrated by Tina Holdcroft

Jaap Tuinman

CONSULTANTS

Sharon Anderson
Elaine Baker
Maxine Bone
Jill Hamilton
Diana Hill
Orysia Hull
Sandy Johnstone
Moira Juliebö
Beverley Kula
Helen Langford
Mary Neeley
Carol Pfaff
Sharon Rich

PROGRAM EDITOR
Kathleen Doyle

Ginn Publishing Canada Inc.

JOURNEYS

Level Three
Watch Out, Freddy, Muffles, and Percy!

© Copyright 1990 by Ginn Publishing
Canada Inc.
ALL RIGHTS RESERVED.
No part of this publication may be
reproduced or transmitted in any
form or by any means, electronic,
photographic, or mechanical, or
by any information storage and
retrieval system, without the prior
written permission of the publisher.

C99134
ISBN 0-7702-1704-4

Printed and bound in Canada.
ABCDEFG   96543210

Muffles and the Hat

The wind went WHOOSH! and blew
Muffles's hat off her head.
"My hat!" said Muffles Mole, and ran
after it.

Muffles ran BAM! into Percy Pig.
"Watch out, Muffles!" he said.
"My hat!" said Muffles. "The wind
blew my hat away."
"I'll help you get it," said Percy.
And the two of them ran after
the hat.

4

Muffles and Percy ran BAM! into Freddy
Frog.

"Look out, you two," said Freddy.

"Come on, Freddy," they said.
"Help us get that hat."

And the three of them ran
after the hat.

"Look," said Freddy. "Your hat's up in the tree."

Muffles went up the tree, but she couldn't reach the hat.

Muffles started to cry.

"Don't cry," said Freddy. "I'll hop up the tree and get your hat."

Then Muffles looked up.

"No, Freddy, don't go up," she said. "See that brown and white bird? It wants to make a nest in my hat. Let the bird have it. It's best as a nest."

Big or Little?

Freddy looked down in the water and saw a frog.

"What a big frog!" said Freddy.

Then Freddy saw that **he** was the big frog.

"Is that me?" said Freddy. "Am I really that big?"

Freddy saw a spider in a web.

"Spider, look at me," said Freddy. "Am I big?"

"Yes," said the spider. "You're big."

Freddy saw some worms in a hole.
"Worms, look at me," said Freddy. "Am I
big?"
"Yes," said the worms. "You're big."

Freddy saw a fox in a field.

"Fox, look at me," said Freddy. "Am I big?"

"Well," said the fox. "You're big for a frog, but you're not as big as I am."

Freddy saw a bear on a log.

"Bear, come and look at me," said Freddy. "The spider says I'm big. The worms say I'm big. But the fox says I'm not as big as he is. What do you say? Am I big?"

13

The bear laughed.

"You are big **and** little," he said. "You look big to the spider and the worms. You look little to the fox. And you look very little to me. But I look little to a whale. All of us are big **and** little."

A Magic Trick

"Freddy and I want to put on a magic show," said Muffles.

"Do you want to be in it?" Freddy asked Percy.

"Yes," said Percy. "What can I do?"

"I know what you can do," said Muffles.
"You can lie down in a box and we'll saw
you in two."

"What?" said Percy. "Saw me in two?"

"It's OK," said Freddy. "It's a magic trick.
We can do it."

"No you can't!" said Percy. "I won't let
you!"

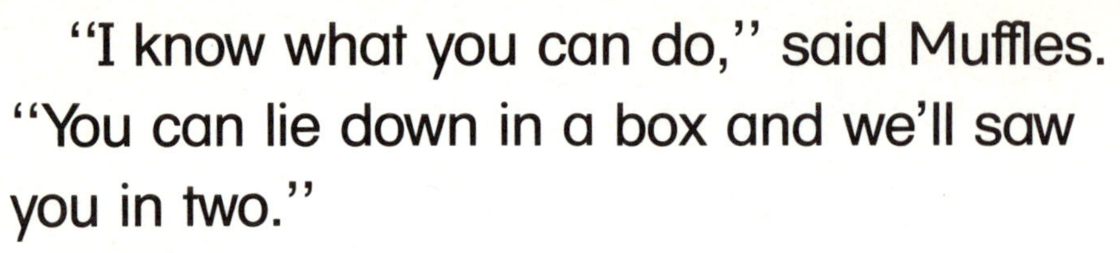

"I know what you can do," said Freddy.
"You can come over here and we'll make
you a purple pig."

"What?" said Percy. "A purple pig?"

"It's OK," said Muffles. "It's a magic trick.
We can do it."

"No you can't," said Percy. "I won't let
you."

"I know what you can do," said Muffles. "You can get in that box and we'll make you go away."

"What?" said Percy. "Make me go away?"

"It's OK," said Muffles. "It's a magic trick. I will tap the box and say 'POOF!' and you will go away. We can do it."

"Yes you can," said Percy. "I know you can."

So Percy got in the box.
"POOF!" said Muffles.

"Percy's gone!" said Freddy. "The magic trick worked!"

"I can do another magic trick," said Muffles. "I can make Percy come back."

"No you can't," whispered Percy. "I won't let you."

20